Fondue

AUTHOR: CLAUDIA LENZ
PHOTOS: FOODARTFACTORY OHG,
KLAUS-MARIA EINWANGER, DANIEL PETRI

Practical Tips

Appendix

Recipes

10 Cheese Fondues

18 Stock and Oil Fondues

40 Sauces, Salads, and Sides

52 Sweet Fondues

Cooking Gear

Cheese, stock, oil, or chocolate; different fondues require different pots in which the contents can melt creamily, simmer gently, or bubble smartly.

Caquelon

Meat fondue pot

Electric fondue set

Caquelon Authentic cheese fondue is prepared in a caquelon or, as the Swiss call it, a Fonduekachel, which is a wide, shallow pot made of earthenware or high-grade steel-ceramic (Silargan). These materials provide excellent insulation and prevent both melted cheese and liquid chocolate from cooling too much around the edges and hardening. They also maintain the high temperature necessary for melting the cheese mixture.

Meat fondue pot The traditional pot for oil and stock fondues is a heat-resistant pot over an open flame. Generations of fondue have brought changes in both materials and heating methods.

Modern fondue pots are made of high-grade steel-ceramic (Silargan), die-cast aluminum, cast iron, or stainless steel. Some of these pots can also be used for cheese fondue. In this case, they should have vertical sides and be made of smooth, robust steel-ceramic.

On the practical side, many fondue pots have a splash guard with notches for holding the forks.

Electric fondue set The past few years have brought changes to what goes on under the pot. Spirit burners are out. They form soot and release pollutants, not to mention that a pot of burning liquid on the dinner table can be extremely dangerous. You're better off using sterno. This fuel made from alcohol is available in bottles or in premeasured aluminum cups that are set inside the burner. Electric fondue pots are completely non-polluting and safe because they lack an open flame. Because their temperature can be continuously adjusted from lukewarm to over 400°F, they're equally suitable for oil, stock, cheese and chocolate fondues.

Cheese: The Original Fondue

The base In its country of origin, cheese fondue is made with melted Swiss and French cheeses, usually a mixture of Gruyère, Emmenthaler, Appenzeller, Vacherin, and Raclette. Mix and match varieties and portions from this large, international assortment.

Cheese

Bread

Wine Wine dissolves and blends. Acid and alcohol are good for melting hard cheese. Select a some-what acidic white wine (see page 64) and/or a little lemon juice. Another way to guarantee that the melted ingredients form a creamy mixture is to stir them constantly, starting with a wire whisk and as the amount of cheese grows, with a mixing spoon. Don't worry if the cheese contains lumps. When you finally stir in a little cornstarch mixed with hard liquor (usually fruit brandy), the cheese will become smooth and creamy.

Wine

For dunking Select breads that aren't crumbly. These are easiest to spear and won't fall apart in the pot. Day-old bread is fine for fondue. It holds the cheese well and can be scraped along the bottom of the pot.

Oil and Stock Fondues

In contrast to cheese fondue, everything is cooked right at the table; simmered in a fine stock or deep-fried in a neutral oil.

Fine stock It's up to you whether you want to make instant stock with bouillon cubes, a canned or concentrated stock, or a home-made, organic vegetable or meat stock. Canned stock can always be refined by adding some wine or cream, herbs, an onion pierced with cloves and bay leaves, or by adding tomatoes or mushrooms. Experiment with different combinations to find what tastes best to you. If you prefer to make your own stock, go for it. Just remember to set aside plenty of time for preparation (see recipe on page 27).

FYI
If you don't have an electric fondue set, heat the oil or stock first on the stovetop. It saves burner fuel and is safer.

Solid fat With an oil fondue, the fondue ingredients are cooked in hot oil, meaning that they're deep-fried. Since the fondue pot gets extremely hot, you need to use fats and oils that can withstand high temperatures, such as coconut and palm oil. Both of these are solid at room temperature and are sold in slabs. Other fats that are highly heat-resistant and also come in bars and cubes are special industrially hardened deep-frying fats. They're a mixture of different vegetable oils and fats. All fats of this type have a neutral flavor, making them ideal for fondue, regardless of whether you are cooking meat, bread, or fruit.

The same is true of heat-resistant clarified butter. With its fine butter flavor, it's excellent for frying foods in batter. If you want the fondue to be especially hearty, you can also use pork, beef, or duck lard.

Good vegetable oils Refined vegetable oils tolerate the high temperatures necessary for oil fondues. Their smoke point is over 400°F (200°C). This means that the first oil components don't start to burn until the temperature exceeds 400°F (200°C). Neutral-tasting, refined canola oil can also be used for your oil fondue. It can be heated to 350°F (180°C).

Refined olive oil is another good way to cook meat and vegetables. If you prefer organic, use cold-pressed organic oils, such as sunflower or peanut oil.

Preparing oil Before you start the fondue, fill the pot no more than two-thirds full of fat or oil. If you use solid deep-frying fat, melt it on the stove over low heat until it turns to liquid. Only then can the temperature reach maximum 350°F (180°C) over high heat. You'll know that it's reached the right temperature when a piece of white bread dropped in the oil quickly turns golden brown. If it doesn't change color, let the oil cook some more before trying to cook any other ingredients, because they'll soak up a lot of oil.

Bouillon cubes and stock

Herbs, onions, and cream

Fats and oils

Keeping oil After each fondue, let the fat or oil cool to below 200°F (100°C) and strain it through a paper coffee filter, preferably an extra-fine coffee filter holder. Store the oil in a cool, dark place until its next use. Reuse deep-frying fat up to six times. If it smells bad or turns dark, discard it.

Discarding oil Old fat goes either to a recycling center or into the garbage—but never down the drain! If you don't deep-fry very often, throw it away. During storage (over 1 month), its quality goes down. Wrap solid fat in newspaper and pour liquid oil into a sealable container.

FYI
Never heat deep-frying fat or oil so hot that it smokes. Smoke is a sure sign that fat components are burning. This means the oil is spoiled and should not be consumed.

TIP
For an oil fondue, supply each guest with a stack of paper towels so they can briefly drain their fried meat, fish, or vegetables before eating them.

It Can All be Cooked in a Fondue Pot

Stock and oil are an ingenious medium for cooking a wide variety of ingredients. It's important that ingredients cook quickly so no one has to wait too long with empty plates!

Poultry In a fondue pot, ingredients are cooked briefly, so poultry pieces must be small and from quality cuts. To emerge tender from the pot, it must be as free of sinews and bones as possible. Chicken (breast or thigh) meat is best skinless when cooked in stock and with skin when cooked in oil. Try cooking thin strips of duck breast for a delicious change from chicken!

Meat For pork, beef, lamb, or game, the fillet or tenderloin is the preferred cut

Fish & Seafood As a general rule, any fish with firm flesh (e.g. salmon, halibut, trout, cod) can be speared with a fork and cooked in oil or stock because it won't fall apart. Always use fresh fish that is raised responsibly.

In the case of seafood, anything that tastes good is allowed, from shrimp and small squid to delicious scallops. Make sure pieces aren't too small or they'll dry out.

TIP
For tender, flat fillets such as flatfish, season or marinate them, then roll them up and secure with a wooden toothpick—now they're ready to be speared.

Vegetables Whether as an accompaniment to meat or fish, or as a purely vegetarian meal, whether in stock, oil, or in batter, virtually any type of vegetable can be cooked in a fondue pot. Firmer vegetables should be precooked until crisp-tender so they don't come out of the pot as "crudités". In cheese fondue, on the other hand, raw vegetables taste great.

Fruit If you cook sweet, juicy fruit in oil without batter choose relatively firm and ripe fruit. Good choices include apples, pears, pineapple, and firm peaches. Anything goes with chocolate fondue. Popular favorites include juicy strawberries, apricot halves, and banana slices. If fresh fruit is not readily available, try using canned or frozen fruit.

Dough You can "bake" in a fondue pot by deep-frying in fat or oil. Try our little choux pastry or yeast-dough cream puffs (recipes on pages 56 and 58). Enjoy your mini-cream puffs with fruit sauces and some whipped cream.

Poultry

Meat

Fish & seafood

Vegetabl

Fruit

Dough and mini cream puffs

Cheese Fondues

Gorgonzola Fondue is easy, doesn't use wine, and can be seasoned in a variety of ways. It can be made as a romantic cheese dinner for two or for a group of friends. In the case of a group, simply multiply the amounts in the recipe, but go easy on the cornstarch.

Creamy Gorgonzola Fondue

3½ oz (100 g) Gorgonzola
   ½ cup (100 ml) milk
   1 teaspoon cornstarch
   1⅗ oz (50 g) mild grated cheese (e.g. Gouda, Edam)

Serves 1 | ⏱ Prep time: 10 minutes
Per serving approx.: 610 calories, 35 g protein, 49 g fat, 7 g carbohydrates

1 Heat and melt Gorgonzola in half the milk. Mash cheese with a whisk and stir.

2 Once cheese has melted, stir cornstarch into a little remaining milk and add to cheese. Briefly bring to a boil while stirring and let thicken.

3 Gradually add grated cheese while stirring. Melt and stir in just enough milk to make cheese mixture creamy.

Serve with olive or herb ciabatta.

VARIATION
Replace part of the milk with strained or chopped tomatoes. Season with dried thyme, oregano, or basil.

basic recipe

Swiss Cheese Fondue

Making cheese fondue is simple. This basic recipe serves as a template for experimenting with different types of cheese and wine and with different brandies, seasonings, and breads.

12oz (350 g) Gruyère
12oz (350 g) Emmenthaler
1 clove garlic (optional)
1½ cup (400 ml) dry white wine
1–2 level tablespoons cornstarch (as desired)
2 tbs (2–4 cl) fruit brandy (as desired)
Freshly grated nutmeg
Freshly ground white pepper
2½ cups (600 g) crusty bread

Serves 4 | ⊙ Prep time: 30 minutes
Per serving approx.: 1180 calories, 63 g protein, 56 g fat, 89 g carbohydrates

1   Grate cheese coarsely. If desired, cut garlic in half, spear each half with a fork, and rub cut edge around the inside of the fondue pot.

2   Pour half the wine into fondue pot and heat on the stove. Gradually add cheese and remaining wine while stirring, first with a wire whisk (Figure 1) and later with a mixing spoon (Figure 2). Keep mixture at the boiling point and stir vigorously until cheese melts and blends with wine. You may have some wine left over, depending on the consistency desired—not too thick, not too runny.

3   Add 1 tablespoon cornstarch to 1 tablespoon brandy and stir until smooth. Add to boiling cheese mixture and briefly bring to a boil while stirring. If desired, stir remaining cornstarch into remaining brandy and use to blend cheese. Remove from heat and season with nutmeg and pepper. Transfer pot to fondue burner and keep mixture at boiling point.

4   Cut bread into bite-sized pieces so that every piece has a crust. With a fondue fork, spear bread from the soft side into crust, dip into cheese, stir, and remove.

5   One by one, dip each piece of bread with warm cheese and enjoy.

Always scrape bread along the bottom of the pot to keep cheese from burning. From time to time, stir cheese mixture thoroughly with a mixing spoon so it doesn't separate.

MORE OR FEWER PEOPLE AT THE TABLE?
Count on 5½ oz (150 g) of cheese per person. Some recipes even call for up to 10½ oz (300 g) cheese. When up to 6 people are sticking their forks into the pot, it should still contain enough melted cheese so that everyone can dip, stir, and enjoy right down to the last bite.

delicious with rye bread

Cheese and Bacon Fondue

1 small onion | 1¼ lb (600 g) Butterkäse cheese (found in gourmet food stores or online) | 2 oz (50 g) finely diced bacon | ½ cup (125 g) strained tomatoes | ⅓ cup (75 ml) hearty white wine | 1 tablespoon cornstarch | 3 tablespoons milk | Hungarian sweet paprika | Kosher Salt | Freshly ground white pepper | Dried marjoram

Serves 4 | ⏲ Prep time: 25 minutes
Per serving approx.: 1000 calories, 39 g protein, 60 g fat, 73 g carbohydrates

1   Peel onion and chop finely. Grate cheese coarsely. Place fondue pot on the stove and fry bacon and onions over low heat until translucent. Add tomatoes and wine. Gradually add cheese while stirring with a mixing spoon until melted (see Basic Recipe, page 13).

2   Whisk cornstarch into milk and add to pot. Briefly bring to a boil while stirring and let thicken. Season to taste with paprika, salt, pepper, and marjoram.

slightly tart

Brie Fondue

1 clove garlic, peeled | 1⅓ lb (750 g) young brie (weight without rind) | 1¾ cups (450 ml) hard cider | 2 tablespoons lemon juice |1 tbsp (15 g) flour | Medium-hot mustard | Freshly ground white pepper

Serves 4 | ⏲ Prep time: 20 minutes
Per serving approx.: 1010 calories, 51 g protein, 50 g fat, 81 g carbohydrates

1   Cut garlic in half, spear halves with a fork and rub around the inside of the fondue pot. Cut cheese into very small pieces. Combine cider and lemon juice.

2   Add cheese and all but 3 tablespoons cider to the fondue pot and place pot on the stove. Melt cheese over medium heat while stirring and blend (see Basic Recipe, page 13). Stir flour into remaining cider, add to cheese, bring to a boil while stirring and let thicken. Season to taste with mustard and pepper.

If desired, serve with zucchini cubes, fresh mushrooms, and bread for dipping.

nutty & tangy

Cheshire Fondue

2½ oz (75 g) hazelnuts | 1¼ lb (600 g) Cheshire cheese | 1 clove garlic | 2 tbsp butter | ⅓ cup (100 ml) milk | 1⅔ cups (400 ml) white wine (e.g. Gewürztraminer) | 1 tbs cornstarch | 1 tbs (2–4 cl) apricot brandy | Freshly ground white pepper

Serves 4 | ⏲ Prep time: 30 minutes
Per serving approx.: 1245 calories, 53 g protein, 66 g fat, 91 g carbohydrates

1 Grind hazelnuts finely. Grate cheese coarsely. Peel garlic and mince.

2 Place fondue pot on the stove and heat butter until it begins to foam. Braise garlic and nuts until golden brown.

3 Alternately add milk, cheese, and wine while stirring. Melt cheese and blend (see Basic Recipe, page 13). Stir cornstarch into brandy, stir brandy into cheese mixture and briefly bring to a boil. Season to taste with pepper.

delicious with pretzels

Cheese and Beer Fondue

½ bunch Italian parsley | 1¼ lb (600 g) Tilsit cheese with caraway seeds | ¼ cup freshly squeezed lemon juice | 1⅓ cup (300 ml) Pilsner beer | 1 tbs cornstarch | 3 tbs (4 cl) whiskey | Ground ginger

Serves 4 | ⏲ Prep time: 25 minutes
Per serving approx.: 890 calories, 47 g protein, 41 g fat, 70 g carbohydrates

1 Rinse parsley, shake dry and chop leaves. Grate cheese coarsely. Add cheese and lemon juice to fondue pot and melt over low heat while stirring.

2 Continue stirring while gradually adding beer then bring to a boil. Stir cornstarch into whiskey until smooth then stir whiskey into cheese mixture.

3 Briefly bring to a boil while stirring. Season to taste with ginger and sprinkle with parsley before serving.

colorful and healthy

Cheese Fondue with Potatoes and Vegetables

With many different ingredients for dipping, this basic recipe is ideal for large groups.

Dipping ingredients
1¾ lbs (800 g) firm potatoes
2 tbs extra virgin olive oil
Kosher salt
Freshly ground pepper
Hungarian sweet paprika
4 cups (1 liter) vegetable stock
1¾ lb (800 g) assorted vegetables (e.g. cauliflower, broccoli, carrots, mushrooms, bell peppers, fennel, celery)
Parchment paper

For the fondue
1¾ lbs (800 g) Emmenthaler (or Gouda)
2 onions
1 bunch Italian parsley
½ cup (100 g) butter
About 2 cups (500 ml) milk
2 tbs cornstarch
Freshly ground white pepper

Serves 6 | 🕐 Prep time: 50 minutes | Baking time: about 50 minutes
Per serving approx.: 865 calories, 47 g protein, 61 g fat, 30 g carbohydrates

1 Preheat oven to 350°F (180°C). Brush potatoes thoroughly under running water, pat dry and cut lengthwise into quarters with or without the peel. In a wide bowl, combine olive oil, salt, pepper, and paprika. Dredge potatoes in this mixture and place on a baking sheet lined with parchment paper. Bake on the middle oven rack for 40–50 minutes until golden brown.

2 Heat stock. Separate or cut vegetables into bite-sized pieces. Cook carrots and fennel in stock for 8–10 minutes until crisp-tender. After 5 minutes, add cauliflower or broccoli and, if desired, celery and cook for about 3 minutes until crisp-tender. Plunge vegetables into cold water and drain. Arrange on serving dishes.

3 Grate cheese coarsely. Peel onions and mince. Rinse parsley, pat dry, and chop leaves finely. Melt butter in fondue pot and braise onions with half the parsley over low heat until translucent. Gradually add 1 cup (250 ml) milk and cheese while stirring with a mixing spoon and melt, keeping mixture at the boiling point. Add cornstarch to ¼ cup (5 tablespoons) milk, stir into cheese mixture and briefly bring to a boil. Add remaining milk to thin. The mixture should be combined and smooth but not too thick or the potatoes and vegetables will fall off the fork too easily. If necessary, add a little more milk. Season to taste with pepper and sprinkle with remaining parsley.

4 Transfer pot to fondue burner. Remove potatoes from oven, place in a serving bowl and serve with vegetables.

Stock and Oil Fondues

Both fondues are quick to prepare and the ingredients are easy to buy and relatively inexpensive. The recipe here is for meat but can be substituted as desired with pickled vegetables, carrot and celery sticks, and raw vegetable pieces that are speared and cooked in the stock. Serving with dips and sauces also adds to this meal.

Meat Medley

1 cup (250 ml) beef stock
½ cup (125 ml) white wine (optional)
1 onion studded with 2 cloves
2 bay leaves
Bunch of mixed herbs (e.g. tarragon,
  thyme, parsley)
14 oz (400 g) pork tenderloin
14 oz (400 g) mild, smoked sausage
14 oz (400 g) pork bratwurst
Kosher salt
Freshly ground pepper

Serves 4 | ⏱ Prep time: 20 minutes
Per serving approx.: 785 calories, 51 g protein,
64 g fat, 0 g carbohydrates

1 Combine stock, wine, studded onion, bay leaf,
and herbs as desired in the fondue pot. Place pot
on stove, cover, bring to a boil, and simmer for
about 10 minutes.

2 Thinly slice pork tenderloin and sausage into
pieces 1 inch (2-3 cm) long. Squeeze sausage out
of bratwurst skins and shape into balls. Arrange
everything on serving dishes. Transfer stock to the
fondue burner, and start cooking!

GOES WITH?
Herb dip: Stir together 3/4 cup (200 g) sour cream,
1–2 tablespoons mustard (depending on spiciness),
1 teaspoon chopped tarragon or 1 tablespoon chopped
dill, salt, and pepper. Prepare sauces as desired (see
recipes beginning on page 41).

with fine ham | lightly spicy

Beef Fondue with Tomato Stock

Here's something different: Use tomato stock for cooking beef and zucchini slices wrapped in Parma ham. Finish up by drinking a stunningly seasoned stock.

Dipping ingredients
½ lb (250 g) asparagus
Kosher salt
¼ lb (100 g) snow peas
1 cup (250 g) cherry tomatoes
1¼ lb (300 g) beef tenderloin
1 small, thin zucchini
⅔ lb (300 g) finely sliced Parma ham

For the stock
1 clove garlic
1 onion
2 tbs oil
1⅔ cups (400 ml) hearty beef stock
3½ cups (800 g) chopped tomatoes
3 sprigs fresh oregano
3 sprigs fresh thyme
2 tbs Parmagiano-Reggiano
1 tsp lemon zest

Serves 4 | ⏲ Prep time: 40 minutes
Per serving approx.: 465 calories, 60 g protein, 29 g fat, 18 g carbohydrates

1   Rinse asparagus, clean, peel bottom third, and cook in boiling salted water for about 8 minutes until crisp-tender. Remove from water and cut into bite-sized pieces. Rinse snow peas, clean, and cook in asparagus water for 5 minutes until crisp-tender. Rinse tomatoes.

2   Slice beef into bite-sized pieces. Rinse zucchini, clean, and slice into ¼ inch (½ cm) thick pieces. Wrap 1 slice ham around each zucchini slice. Arrange vegetables and meat on serving dishes.

3   Peel garlic and onion and mince. In the fondue pot, heat oil on the stove and braise garlic and onion until translucent. Add oregano, thyme, and chopped tomatoes, bring to a boil and simmer for about 5 minutes.

4   Remove herbs. Stir in Parmagiano-Reggiano and season with lemon zest. Transfer pot with stock to the fondue burner and cook ingredients to desired doneness.

TIP—FOR A HEARTY SOUP
After the fondue, don't throw away the stock! It's loaded with nutrients and flavor-giving ingredients. The next day, add a little cream and cooked soup noodles, as desired, to make a delicious soup appetizer.

takes time to prepare

Sausage Fondue

For the stock
1¾ cups (400 ml) veal stock | 1¾ cups (400 ml) vegetable stock | ¾ cup (200 g) cream | ½ cup (125 g) crème fraîche | ½ bunch Italian parsley | 3–4 tablespoons medium-hot mustard | 1–2 tablespoons Dijon mustard | Kosher salt | Freshly ground pepper
Plus
3 onions | ½ cup (125 g) softened butter | 1¾ lbs (800 g) mixed cooked sausages (e.g. bockwurst, frankfurters, hotdogs, Regensburger, Lyon) | 4 pretzel sticks | 8 oz jar (250 g) kosher pickle slices

Serves 4 | 🕐 Prep time: 35 minutes
Per serving approx.: 1190 calories, 33 g protein, 106 g fat, 18 g carbohydrates

1 In the fondue pot, combine stocks, cream, and crème fraîche. Bring to a boil on the stove, uncover, and reduce by about one-fourth.

2 In the meantime, peel and chop onions. Heat 3 tablespoons butter and brown onions while stirring. Mix with remaining butter and refrigerate. Rinse parsley, shake dry, and chop leaves. Slice sausages into ½ inch (1–2 cm) pieces.

3 Stir mustard into reduced stock and simmer for several minutes. Season with salt and pepper. Transfer to the fondue burner and heat sausage pieces in mustard stock. Spread pretzel sticks with onion butter and eat with pickles.

also delicious with eel

Fish in Beer

2 cups (500 ml) light-colored beer | 1 vegetable bouillon cube | 1 teaspoon caraway seeds | 3 teaspoons pink peppercorns | 1 bay leaf | 1½ tbs (25 g) flour | 1½ tbs (25 g) softened butter | Turmeric | Kosher salt | Freshly ground pepper | 1¾ lbs (800 g) fish fillet (e.g. sea bass, halibut, flounder, swordfish, tuna, catfish, eel) cut into bite-sized pieces

Serves 4 | 🕐 Prep time: 35 minutes
Per serving approx.: 260 calories, 35 g protein, 9 g fat, 3 g carbohydrates

1 In the fondue pot, combine beer, 4 cups (1 liter) water, bouillon cube, caraway seeds and peppercorns. Crumble bay leaf coarsely and add. Bring to a boil and simmer for 10 minutes. In the meantime, knead together flour and butter.

2 Pour 1 cup (250 ml) of beer stock into a saucepan. Keep stock hot in fondue pot. Bring to a boil and add flour-butter bit by bit while beating vigorously. Simmer over low heat for 10 minutes but do not boil. Season with turmeric, salt, and pepper. Keep warm at the table on a tea warmer.

3 Transfer pot with hot stock to fondue burner. Adjust temperature so that stock doesn't boil. Simmer fish in stock until done, dip into hot sauce, and enjoy!

Serve with small, new potatoes, green salad, and cucumber salad.

exquisite | for holidays

Game Fondue with Cranberry Sauce

Thanks to modern game preserves and because frozen game has long been available, this special fondue can be enjoyed whatever the season.

2¼ lbs (1 kg) mixed game fillet (e.g. saddle of venison, wild boar,)

For the stock
1 oz (30 g) dried porcini mushrooms
3⅓ cups (800 ml) game or chicken stock
1 clove garlic
1 bay leaf
4 allspice berries
1 small bunch Italian parsley

For the sauce
¼ cup (60 g) cranberry jam
⅓ cup (100 g) sour cream
Kosher salt
Ground allspice

Serves 4 | ⏱ Prep time: 50 minutes
Per serving approx.: 360 calories, 56 g protein, 11 g fat, 8 g carbohydrates

1   For the stock, place mushrooms in a strainer, rinse under cold water, and drain. In a small saucepan, bring ¾ cup (200 ml) stock to a boil, remove from heat, and soak mushrooms for at least 20 minutes.

2   In the meantime, use a sharp knife to remove all bits of skin and sinews from the game, cut into bite-sized pieces, cover, and set aside.

3   Pour remaining stock into fondue pot and bring to a boil. Peel garlic and cut in half. Crumble bay leaf. Add garlic, bay leaf, and allspice berries to stock. Rinse parsley, chop only the coarse stems into small pieces, and add to stock. Use remaining parsley elsewhere (see "Goes with?" below). Pour mushroom liquid through a fine strainer and add to fondue pot. Slice mushrooms into small pieces and add. Cover stock and simmer for 15 minutes.

4   For the sauce, stir together cranberry jam and sour cream and season generously to taste with salt and allspice.

GOES WITH?
Prepare at least two additional sauces as desired, Parsley Salsa (page 43) or Egg Sauce (page 41), both go well with game. Use leftover parsley to make the salsa. Serve with raw vegetables or salad.

VARIATION
Serve with fresh, mushroom filled ravioli. Just place ravioli in the stock, cook until done, and serve alongside game.

mild mushroom aroma

Japanese Stock

1 oz (30 g) dried cloud ear mushrooms | 4 cups
(1 liter) chicken stock | 1 small carrot | 2 oz (50 g)
snow peas | 2 tablespoons light soy sauce |
1 tablespoon sake (or dry white wine) | Kosher
salt | Freshly ground pepper

Makes 4 cups (1 liter) stock | ⏲ Prep time:
35 minutes | Per serving approx.: 45 calories,
5 g protein, 1 g fat, 10 g carbohydrates

1   Simmer mushrooms in stock for 10 minutes.
Rinse and clean vegetables. Peel carrots and cut
into fine matchsticks. Cut snow peas diagonally
into wide strips.

2   Remove mushrooms, let cool briefly, and cut
into thin strips. Add remaining vegetables to stock.
Season with soy sauce, sake, salt, and pepper.
Simmer for 15 minutes and serve.

FOR DIPPING
Beef cubes, snow peas, spinach, chard, Chinese
cabbage leaves, sliced mushrooms, tofu.

hot & spicy

Sangrita Red-Wine Stock

1 cup (250 ml) spicy sangrita | 1 cup (250 ml)
dry red wine | 2 cups (500 ml) beef or vegetable
stock | 2 cloves garlic | 1 green onion | 2 sprigs
thyme | 2 sprigs marjoram | Kosher salt | **Plus:**
Disposable tea filter bag, kitchen string

Makes 4 cups (1 liter) stock | ⏲ Prep time:
25 minutes | Per serving approx.: 95 calories,
0 g protein, 1 g fat, 7 g carbohydrates

1   Combine sangrita, wine, and stock in fondue
pot. Peel garlic and cut in half. Rinse green onion,
clean and chop white part coarsely. Place garlic,
onion, and herbs in the tea filter bag and secure
with kitchen string.

2   Bring all ingredients to a boil and simmer for
about 10 minutes. Remove herb bag and season
with salt to taste.

DIPPING INGREDIENTS
Pork, beef, spicy cooked sausages.

Fine Fish Stock

Ask your fish monger which carcasses and fish pieces are suitable for stock and which fillets are suitable for fondue.

2¼ lb (1 kg) fish carcasses and pieces (without gills or skin) from lean, white fish (e.g. halibut, sea bass, swordfish, cod) | 1 onion | 1 leek | 1 stalk celery | 1 parsley root | 1 small fennel bulb | 1 tbs white peppercorns | 1 tsp salt | 1 bay leaf | 2 sprigs thyme | 2 cups (500 ml) dry white wine

Makes 4–6 cups (1–1½ liters) stock |
⏲ Prep time: 50 minutes
Per serving approx.: 195 calories, 1 g protein, 6 g fat, 6 g carbohydrates

1 Rinse fish carcasses and pieces thoroughly under cold running water to remove all blood and skin residue and place in a large pot. Rinse or peel vegetables, clean and cut into pieces of about 4 inches (10 cm). Add vegetables, peppercorns, salt, bay leaf, and thyme to the pot

2 Add wine and 8 cups (2 liters) cold water. Cover, bring to a boil, and simmer over medium heat for 20 minutes, frequently removing scum from the surface.

3 Pour mixture through a fine strainer lined with a cheesecloth or a kitchen towel. Simmer uncovered and reduce to 4-6 cups (1–1½ liters).

TYPES OF FISH TO DIP...
Dip flatfish such as flounder, halibut, or catfish, plus fillet of monkfish and red snapper. Slice fish fillets and drizzle with olive oil, season with white pepper and chopped tarragon, and marinate for 30 minutes.

GOES WITH?
Aioli, spiced oils, oil pastes such as red or green pesto, and herb butter.

versatile and variable vegetables

Vegetarian Stock Fondue

This pot is colorful and downright healthy, and the hot vegetables are ideal for dipping.

14 oz (400 g) firm tofu

4 tbs oil for frying

2½ lbs (1.2 kg) cleaned vegetables (e.g. Brussels
   sprouts, green beans, bell peppers, celery,
   broccoli, cauliflower, mushrooms, zucchini)

For the stock

1 cup (250 ml) white wine (may substitute water)

3 cups (750 ml) hearty vegetable stock

¾ cup (200 ml) heavy cream

1 clove garlic

Several sprigs fresh herbs (e.g. Italian parsley,
   oregano, thyme)

2–3 tbs cornstarch

1 tsp lemon juice

Kosher salt

Serves 4 | ⏱ Prep time: 40 minutes
Per serving approx.: 315 calories, 15 g protein,
22 g fat, 12 g carbohydrates

1 Pat tofu dry and cut into cubes of about ½ inch
(1–2 cm). Heat oil and sauté tofu on all sides over
medium heat, turning occasionally.

2 Blanch all vegetables except mushrooms and
zucchini in boiling salted water for about 5 minutes
until crisp-tender. Plunge into cold water and drain.

3 For the stock, combine ¾ cup (200 ml) wine,
vegetable stock, and cream in fondue pot. Peel
garlic and mince. Add garlic and herbs to pot, bring
to a boil, and simmer for 10 minutes. Remove

herbs. Stir cornstarch into remaining wine and add
to simmering stock while stirring. Briefly bring to
a boil and let thicken. Season to taste with lemon
juice and salt. Transfer to the fondue burner.

4 Separate or cut vegetables into bite-sized
pieces: Slice Brussels sprouts into smaller pieces,
slice beans crosswise into thirds or quarters,
slice bell peppers into strips or diamonds, slice
celery into pieces, and mushrooms and zucchini
into slices about ¼ inch (½ cm) thick. Arrange
vegetables and tofu on serving dishes. Don't
spear too many vegetables at once and cook in
simmering stock.

GOES WITH?
Crusty baguette, sauces as desired, e.g. Herb Sauce,
Egg Sauce, Mustard Sauce (recipes begin on page 41),
horseradish sauce, and chopped nuts, seeds, or
slivered almonds for sprinkling.

TIP
Garnish vegetables with a combination of chopped fresh
herbs , e.g. chervil, parsley, basil, and chives or cress.

VARIATION
Prepare an Asian stock with coconut milk instead of
cream. Flavor with ½ stalk lemon grass (pounded flat),
1–2 dried chili peppers and 1–2 stalks Thai basil.

basic recipe
Beef and Pork Fondue

For procrastinators: Forget the marinade but be sure to pat the beef especially dry before presenting to dip in oil.

1 tsp black peppercorns
1 tsp mustard seeds
1 tsp allspice berries
1 small dried chili pepper
2 tsp (100 ml) vegetable oil
1 bay leaf
2 onions
2¼–2½ lb (1–1.2 kg) lean, beef and pork (e.g. beef fillet or tenderloin, pork tenderloin)
Oil for deep-frying

Serves 4 | ⏲ Prep time: 30 minutes |
Marinating time: 12 hours
Per serving approx.: 400 calories, 53 g protein, 21 g fat, 0 g carbohydrates

1 For the marinade, briefly toast peppercorns, mustard seeds, and allspice berries in an ungreased pan until they give off an aroma. Crush seasonings with chili pepper in a mortar.

2 In a small saucepan, heat vegetable oil, add seasonings, and simmer for about 4 minutes. Crumble bay leaf, add, and simmer for another minute. Let oil cool and pour through a coffee filter.

3 Peel onions and cut into thin rings. Arrange half in a large casserole dish. Pat meat dry with paper towels, cut into cubes of about ¾ inches (2 cm), mix with seasoned oil and distribute over onions. Cover meat with remaining onions, cover dish, and marinate overnight in the refrigerator.

4 The next day, fill fondue pot three-quarters full and heat on stovetop to about 325°F (170°C) (see page 7). Transfer pot to fondue burner. Remove onions and meat from marinade and arrange in serving dishes.

5 Spear meat with a fork, dip into hot oil and fry until desired doneness is reached. Continuously test the first pieces until you have a feel for the cooking time and temperature. Be careful not to put too much meat in the pot as the oil will cool too much and the meat, instead of frying, will soak up the oil. If this happens, stop cooking, and re-heat oil before dipping meat again.

6 Season meat with salt and pepper on your plate and dip in sauces as desired (see recipes beginning on page 41).

GOES WITH?
Various sauces, vegetables, and a crusty baguette.

TIP
Use the same method to marinate and deep-fry firm, lean fish (e.g. cod, halibut) or medium-sized or large shrimp.

sophisticated & spicy

Dark Meat Fondue

14 oz (400 g) ostrich steak (fresh or frozen and thawed) | 14 oz (400 g) lamb fillet | 7 oz (200 g) beef tenderloin | Oil for deep-frying

For the marinade

1 tbs black peppercorns | 2 cloves garlic | 1 tsp Kosher salt | 3 tbs extra virgin olive oil | 1 tbs finely grated peel from 1 lemon | ½ tsp sambal oelek | 1 tsp dried thyme | ½ tsp ground rosemary

Serves 4 | ⏱ Prep time: 20 minutes | Marinating time: 3 hours
Per serving approx.: 505 calories, 56 g protein, 32 g fat, 1 g carbohydrates

1   Slice meat into bite-sized pieces. For the marinade, crush peppercorns coarsely in a mortar. Peel garlic, chop coarsely, and crush finely with salt. Combine with olive oil, pepper, lemon peel, sambal oelek, thyme, and rosemary.

2   Toss meat with marinade, cover, and refrigerate for at least 3 hours.

3   Place fat or oil in fondue pot and heat on the stove to about 325°F (170°C) (see page 7). Pat oil from meat with paper towels and arrange on serving dishes.

marinated with twice the spices

Poultry Fondue

1¼ lb (600 g) chicken breast fillet | 1 lb 2 oz (500 g) turkey breast fillet | Oil for deep-frying

For the marinade

10 basil leaves | 3 green onions | 1 piece fresh ginger (about 1 inch (2–3 cm) | ⅓ cup (80 ml) extra virgin olive oil | 3 cloves garlic | 1 orange | 5 white peppercorns

Serves 4 | ⏱ Prep time: 20 minutes | Marinating time: 3 hours
Per serving approx.: 520 calories, 64 g protein, 28 g fat, 0 g carbohydrates

1   Chop basil coarsely. Rinse green onions, clean, and chop. Peel ginger and chop finely. Combine basil, green onions, and ginger with half the oil. Peel garlic and slice finely. Rinse orange under hot water, dry, and finely grate half the peel. Crush peppercorns coarsely. Combine garlic, orange peel, and remaining oil.

2   Rinse chicken and turkey, pat dry, and slice into bite-sized pieces. Toss chicken in basil-ginger marinade and toss turkey in garlic-orange marinade. Cover and refrigerate for at least 3 hours.

3   Place oil in fondue pot and heat on the stove to about 325°F (170°C) (see page 7). Pat oil from meat and arrange on serving dishes.

Serve with crusty bread, spicy fruit sauces, herb sauce, vegetables, and green salads.

top: Poultry Fondue | bottom: Dark Meat Fondue

with Asian sauces and sour cream

Spicy Hot Fondue

For the meatballs
1 piece fresh ginger (about 1½ inches (4 cm)) |
2 cloves garlic | Kosher salt | 2 green onions |
14 oz (400 g) ground meat (half beef, half pork) |
1 egg | Freshly ground pepper | 1 tsp sambal oelek
Plus
1½ lb (800 g) hot spicy chicken wings (frozen
and thawed) | Oil for deep-frying | Wire ladle

Serves 4 | ⊚ Prep time: 25 minutes
Per serving approx.: 630 calories, 32 g protein,
55 g fat, 1 g carbohydrates

1 Peel ginger and grate finely (about 3 tablespoons). Peel garlic, mince, and sprinkle with a
little salt. Rinse green onions, mince white part,
and chop green part into rings.

2 Knead together ground meat, ginger, garlic,
green onions, and egg, and season generously
with pepper and sambal oelek. Shape into 20–30
slightly flattened balls.

3 Place fondue pot on stovetop and heat oil to
325°F (170°C) (see page 7). Transfer to fondue
burner. Using a slotted spoon, place meatballs in
oil and fry while turning until brown and crispy.
Spear chicken wings with fondue forks and fry.

TIP—FOR THE CHICKEN WINGS
Spicy frozen chicken wings are available in your super-
market's frozen food section. If desired, spread wings
with a paste made up of 4 garlic cloves crushed with
salt, 1 teaspoon sambal oelek, 2 tablespoons tomato
paste, and 4 tablespoons oil.

must be tried!

Duck Breast Fondue

1½ lb (700g) Barbary duck breast | 7 oz (200 g)
small shallots | 2 small tart apples (e.g. granny
smith) | Oil for deep-frying

Serves 4 | ⊚ Prep time: 20 minutes
Per serving approx.: 700 calories, 35 g protein,
58 g fat, 11 g carbohydrates

1 Rinse duck breast under cold water, pat dry, and
cut crosswise into thin slices.

2 Peel shallots and cut in half lengthwise. Rinse
apples, cut into quarters, remove cores, and cut
quarters crosswise into slices about ¼ inch
(½ cm) thick.

3 Place fondue pot on stovetop and heat oil to
325°F (170°C) (see page 7). Transfer to fondue
burner. Spear duck breast, apples, and onions with
fondue forks and fry until crispy.

SUBSTITUTION TIP
Instead of shallots, use pickled cocktail onions, just pat
dry and fry.

GOES WITH?
Green salad and sauces as desired (recipes begin on
page 41).

easy to vary | with a crispy batter

Tempura Vegetables

With vegetables, there are many choices. This fondue features blanched snow peas and carrot slices, Jerusalem artichokes and parsley root.

1 cup (250 ml) vegetable stock
1 lb (450 g) broccoli
1 red bell pepper
1 yellow bell pepper
14 oz (400 g) zucchini
3 oz (100 g) small brown mushrooms
Vegetable oil for deep-frying

For the batter
2 tbs (30 g) butter
⅔ cup (150 g) flour
⅔ cup (150 ml) dry white wine
Freshly grated nutmeg
Cayenne pepper
Kosher salt
Freshly ground pepper
2 egg whites

Serves 4 | ⊚ Prep time: 40 minutes
Per serving approx.: 490 calories, 11 g protein,
32 g fat, 33 g carbohydrates

1 In a pot, bring stock to a boil. Rinse broccoli and blanch in stock for 5–8 minutes until crisp-tender. Rinse bell peppers, remove seeds, and slice into bite sized pieces. Rinse zucchini and slice into ¼ inch (½ cm) pieces. Clean mushrooms.

2 Drain broccoli (save stock for another purpose) and separate into florets. Peel stems and slice thinly.

3 For the batter, melt butter and let cool. Stir butter, flour, and wine until smooth then season with 1 pinch nutmeg, cayenne pepper, salt, and pepper. Beat egg whites until stiff and fold in. Transfer batter to two serving bowls.

4 Place fondue pot on stovetop and heat oil to 350°F (180°C) (see page 7). Transfer to fondue burner. Spear some of the vegetables with fondue forks, dredge in batter, and fry in hot oil.

VARIATION
Rinse tiny new potatoes, cook with skin on for 20 minutes until crisp-tender, and transfer to serving bowls. At the table, spear potatoes with fondue forks, dredge in batter and fry until crispy.

GOES WITH?
Sauces and dips as desired. We like Arugula Mascarpone Cream. For this dip, rinse a handful of arugula. Peel 1–2 cloves garlic. Purée arugula and garlic with ¼ cup (4 tablespoons) extra virgin olive oil. Stir into ⅔ cup (150 g) Mascarpone, adding just enough milk to make the dip creamy. Season to taste with 1–2 teaspoons lemon juice and 1 teaspoon lemon zest.

crispy classic

Seafood Tempura

For the batter
¼ cup (60 g) flour | ½ cup (125 g) cornstarch |
1 tsp ground ginger | ½ tsp Kosher salt |
Freshly ground pepper
Dipping ingredients
10½ oz (300 g) Savoy cabbage leaves | 10½ oz
(300 g) shiitake mushrooms | 14 oz (400 g)
medium-sized, raw, peeled shrimp (fresh or
frozen) | 14 oz (400 g) firm fish fillet (e.g. halibut,
salmon, fresh or frozen) | Flour for dredging |
Oil for deep-frying | Wire ladle

Serves 4 | ◎ Prep time: 35 minutes
Per serving approx.: 920 calories, 50 g protein,
41 g fat, 98 g carbohydrates

1 Combine flour, cornstarch, ginger, salt, and
pepper and gradually add enough cold water to
make a thick batter. Let stand.

2 Rinse cabbage leaves and blanch in boiling
salted water. Remove from water, plunge into cold
water, drain, and slice coarsely. Clean mushrooms.

3 If necessary, remove vein from shrimp (cut along
the back with a sharp knife and use the tip of the
blade to loosen and pull out vein). Cut fish into
bite-sized pieces. Dust vegetables, shrimp, and
fish with flour (see Tip). Heat oil. Dredge fish and
vegetables in batter and fry.

mild in a tart batter

Turkey in Turmeric Beer Batter

10½ oz (300 g) white mushrooms | Juice from
½ lemon | Kosher salt | Freshly ground pepper |
1¾ lb (800 g) turkey breast fillet | 10½ oz
(300 g) cauliflower florets | Flour for dusting |
Oil for deep-frying
For the batter
¾ cup (180 g) flour | 1 tsp Kosher salt | 1 tsp
turmeric | ¾ cup (175 ml) light-colored beer
(not Pilsner) | ¼ cup (4 tbs) melted butter |
2 egg yolks

Serves 4 | ◎ Prep time: 30 minutes
Per serving approx.: 750 calories, 59 g protein,
39 g fat, 37 g carbohydrates

1 Clean mushrooms, drizzle with lemon juice, and
season with salt and pepper. Cut turkey breast into
cubes of about ¾ inch (2 cm). Dust mushrooms
and turkey on all sides with flour (see Tip) then
arrange on a serving platter.

2 For the beer batter, combine flour, salt, and
turmeric. Add beer, butter, and egg yolks, and stir
together to form a smooth, not-too-runny batter.

3 Place fondue pot on stovetop and heat oil
then transfer to fondue burner. Spear ingredients
individually on fondue forks, dredge in batter and
deep-fry in oil.

Serve with soy sauce and Hot Chili Cucumber Salad
(recipe on page 51).

TIP—FLOURING
Shake vegetables gently in a large strainer while simul-
taneously dusting with a small strainer full of flour until
vegetables are floured on all sides.

Sauces, Salads, and Sides

This first salad is mild but aromatic and goes with almost everything on the fondue table. Egg Salad is a well-loved classic and repeated attempts to substitute it for what are supposedly more exciting, trendy salads have been foiled by the vehement objections of family and friends.

Egg Salad

3 eggs
3 tbs extra virgin olive oil
⅓ cup (6 tbs) heavy cream
2–3 tbs lemon juice
2 tbs medium-hot or hot mustard
Sugar
Kosher salt
Freshly ground pepper
½ bunch chives

Serves 4 | ⊚ Prep time: 25 minutes
Per serving approx.: 220 calories, 6 g protein,
21 g fat, 2 g carbohydrates

1 Boil eggs for 12 minutes, plunge into cold water
and peel. Cut in half, remove yolks, and mash. Mix
with oil, cream, and lemon juice until smooth.

2 Chop egg whites and add to yolks. Season
generously with mustard, sugar, salt, and pepper
and refrigerate for 10 minutes. Rinse chives, shake
dry, chop into fine rings, and stir into sauce.

VARIATION
Instead of chives, try dill, or a Mediterranean herb
mixture. As for the mustard, use whatever you like, with
the exception of sweet mustard.

spicy hot

Tomato Anchovy Dip

Tastes like sea and sun, and is especially good with pork.

½ cup (125 g) chopped canned tomatoes | ¼ cup (4 tbs) extra virgin olive oil | ¼ cup (4 tbs) medium-hot mustard | 2 anchovies in oil + 2 tbs of the oil | 1 large onion | 6 sprigs Italian parsley | 1–2 tbs tomato paste | Sugar | Kosher salt | Freshly ground pepper | Hungarian hot paprika

Serves 6–8 (1 cup or ¼ liter) | ⏱ Prep time: 10 minutes
Per serving approx.: 95 calories, 1 g protein, 10 g fat, 1 g carbohydrates

1 Combine tomatoes, oil, and mustard. Chop anchovies finely. Peel onion and mince. Rinse parsley, shake dry, and chop leaves.

2 Stir anchovies, onion, and parsley into tomato mixture and add tomato paste as desired to make sauce creamier. Season with a little sugar, salt, pepper, and lots of paprika.

VARIATION
Small capers or finely chopped green olives lend a pleasant acidity to this sauce. If desired, add some minced garlic for an extra bite and substitute parsley with dill, oregano, thyme, or basil.

tartly refreshing

Parsley Salsa

This fresh herb salsa goes well with both meat and vegetables.

⅔ cup (150 g) Italian parsley | 2 cloves garlic | 2 shallots | 1 medium pickle | ½ slice sandwich bread | 2 tbs aged balsamic vinegar | ½ cup (125 g) plain yogurt | ½ cup (125 ml) extra virgin olive oil | ½ tsp Kosher salt | Freshly ground white pepper

Serves 6–8 (1 cup or 250 ml) | ⏱ Prep time: 15 minutes
Per serving approx.: 100 calories, 2 g protein, 9 g fat, 4 g carbohydrates

1 Rinse parsley, shake dry, and chop leaves finely. Peel garlic and shallots. Mince garlic and chop shallots and pickle.

2 Cut bread into small cubes. Combine parsley, garlic, shallots, pickle, vinegar, and yogurt. Season generously with salt and pepper, slowly stir in oil and whisk until sauce has emulsified and is creamy.

VARIATION
For an especially striking flavor, replace one-third of the parsley with chervil. For less acidity, replace pickle with grated cucumber. Instead of yogurt, use Mascarpone or sour cream, and stir in a little milk until creamy.

Mixed Green Salad

This fresh, colorful salad can be varied according to the season. Delicious with both cheese and meat fondues.

14 oz (400 g) assorted lettuce leaves (e.g. iceberg, hearts of romaine, radicchio, frisée, chicory, mâche, arugula) | 2 small carrots | 8 medium radishes | 1 small can corn, drained | ½ small box of cress
For the vinaigrette:
1 tbs vegetable stock | 1 tbs mild white vinegar | 2 tbs extra virgin olive oil | 1 tsp mustard | Kosher salt | Freshly ground pepper | ½ bunch Italian parsley

Serves 4 | 🕙 Prep time: 25 minutes
Per serving approx.: 130 calories, 4 g protein, 7 g fat, 12 g carbohydrates

1   Rinse lettuce leaves, spin dry, and tear into bite-sized pieces. Rinse carrots and radishes and clean. Peel carrots and slice finely. In a bowl, toss corn and lettuce.

2   Combine stock, vinegar, oil, and mustard and season generously with salt and pepper. Rinse parsley, shake dry, chop leaves finely and add.

3   Toss lettuce with dressing. Cut cress from bed and scatter over salad.

VARIATION
Refine this sauce with cream, sour cream, or yogurt. Season generously to taste with minced garlic and finely diced shallots or grated horseradish or ginger. Sprouts also make a tasty addition (e.g. bean, sunflower seed, alfalfa or a mixture). If using spicy sprouts, leave out herbs.

Bell-Pepper Horseradish Dip

3½ oz (100 g) pickled roasted bell peppers |
3½ oz (100 g) cream cheese | 2 tsp horseradish
cream | Kosher salt | Freshly ground pepper |
1 pinch ground rosemary

Serves 4 (¾ cup or 175 ml) | ⊕ Prep time:
5 minutes
Per serving approx.: 50 calories, 4 g protein,
3 g fat, 2 g carbohydrates

Drain bell peppers and pat dry. Purée peppers,
cream cheese, and horseradish. Season generously
with salt, pepper, and rosemary.

GOES WITH?
Fish and meat cooked in a neutral liquid or oil, and
also as a dip with boiled, peeled potatoes. Also enjoy
this tart and spicy dip with cheese fondue, alternately
dipping bread in cheese and bread in Bell-Pepper
Horseradish Dip.

Goat Cheese Dip

5 oz (150 g) goat cheese (e.g. Chavroux) |
¼ cup (50 g) plain yogurt | 2 tbs (20 g) pine nuts
| 8 basil leaves (or dried basil) | Freshly ground
white pepper

Serves 4 (175 ml) | ⊕ Prep time: 5 minutes
Per serving approx.: 150 calories, 9 g protein,
12 g fat, 2 g carbohydrates

Purée goat cheese, yogurt, and pine nuts in a
blender until smooth. Finely chop basil and add.
Season with pepper and let stand for at least
30 minutes before serving.

GOES WITH?
Raw and cooked vegetables such as chicory, radicchio,
celery, tomatoes, and bell peppers.

VARIATION
Substitute walnuts for pine nuts, and replace basil with
a mixture of Mediterranean herbs.

tastes best warm

Chard Spirals

1 onion | 1 piece fresh ginger (about 1 inch or
3 cm) | 5 oz (150 g) fresh chard (or spinach) |
2 tbs extra virgin olive oil | 1 carrot | ½ cup
(100 g) crème fraîche | ½ cup (100 g) low-fat
sour cream | ½ cup (125 ml) milk | ¼ cup (60 ml)
canola oil | 2 medium eggs | ⅔ cup (200 g) whole
wheat flour | 1½ tsp baking powder | Kosher salt
| Freshly ground pepper | Coriander | Cardamom |
Flour | Parchment paper

Makes 12 rolls | ⏱ Prep time: 50 minutes |
Baking time: about 30 minutes
Per serving approx.: 160 calories, 5 g protein,
10 g fat, 12 g carbohydrates

1   Peel onion and chop finely. Peel ginger and
grate finely (about 1 tablespoon). Rinse chard,
clean, and cut into strips. Heat olive oil and braise
onions and ginger. Add chard and braise another
1–2 minutes. Peel carrot and grate finely. Stir crème
fraîche and carrot into chard and season generously
with salt and pepper. Stir together sour cream,
4 tablespoons milk, canola oil and 1 egg. Combine
flour, baking powder, ½ teaspoon salt, and 1 large
pinch each of coriander and cardamom. Gradually
work in sour cream.

2   Preheat oven to 400°F (200°C). Separate
remaining egg. Beat egg white. Roll out dough on a
floured work surface to about 12 x 16 inches (30 x
40 cm). Distribute filling on half and spread the rest
with egg white. Roll up, cut into 12 slices about the
thickness of a finger and place on baking sheet
lined with parchment paper. Whisk together egg
yolk and remaining milk and brush onto rolls. Bake
in the oven (middle rack) for 20–30 minutes.

can prepare in advance

Cheese Muffins

5½ oz (150 g) Swiss cheese | 5½ oz (150 g)
pickles | ¾ cup (175 ml) buttermilk | 3 tbs (50 ml)
canola oil | 1 medium egg | 2 pinches salt | ½ tsp
Hungarian sweet paprika | 2 tsp baking powder |
¾ cup (180 g) whole-wheat flour
Plus
Muffin tin with 12 cups | 12 paper baking cups

Makes 12 muffins | ⏱ Prep time: 45 minutes |
Baking time: about 30 minutes
Per serving approx.: 135 calories, 7 g protein,
7 g fat, 11 g carbohydrates

1   Preheat oven to 350°F (180°C). Place baking
cups in tin. Finely dice cheese and pickles.
Combine buttermilk, oil, and egg.

2   Mix together salt, paprika, baking powder, and
flour. Add cheese and pickle to buttermilk and
quickly stir in flour mixture.

3   Pour batter into cups and bake in the oven
(middle rack) for 20-30 minutes until golden brown.

VARIATIONS

Replace Swiss cheese with Feta and replace pickles with
black olives. This variation is especially delicious with
lamb fondue.

left: Cheese Muffins | right: Chard Spirals

Spicy Carrots

1 lb (450 g) carrots | 1½ cups (375 ml) dry white wine | 2 tbs extra virgin olive oil | 2 tsp sugar | 1 bay leaf | Several white peppercorns | 1 small, dried red chili pepper | 1 bouquet garni (Italian parsley, chervil, thyme)

Serves 4 | ⏱ Prep time: 20 minutes
Per serving approx.: 160 calories, 1 g protein, 6 g fat, 11 g carbohydrates

1 Clean carrots, peel, and slice into pieces about ¼ inch (½ cm) thick.

2 Combine wine, ½ cup (125 ml) water, oil, sugar, bay leaf, pepper, chili pepper, and bouquet garni and bring to a boil. Cover and simmer for 5 minutes. Add carrots and blanch for 8–10 minutes until crisp-tender. Remove from heat and let carrots cool in liquid. Remove from liquid to serve.

VARIATIONS
Instead of chili pepper, boil liquid with sliced ginger. Sprinkle carrots with chopped cilantro.

Pickled Vegetables

1 lb (450 g) firm tomatoes | 1 yellow bell pepper | 1 small onion | 1 piece celery root (about 1 oz or 30 g) | 2 tbs sugar | 2 tbs mustard seeds | 1 pinch nutmeg | 1 pinch cinnamon | 5 cloves | ½ cup (125 ml) white wine vinegar

Serves 8 | ⏱ Prep time: 15 minutes
Per serving approx.: 50 calories, 1 g protein, 1 g fat, 12 g carbohydrates

1 Remove cores from tomatoes, blanch, peel and dice coarsely. Rinse bell pepper, cut in half, remove seeds, and cut into strips. Peel onion and chop. Peel celery root and grate.

2 Combine tomatoes, bell peppers, onion, celery root, sugar, mustard seeds, nutmeg, cinnamon, cloves, and vinegar in a ceramic dish, adding a little water if necessary. Cover and refrigerate for at least 10 days. From time to time, stir gently and season to taste to increase the sweet or sour flavor.

Spinach Salad

¼ cup (60 g) raisins | 3 tbs white balsamic vinegar | ¼ cup (60 g) pine nuts | 2¼ lb (1 kg) baby spinach | 4 cloves garlic | ¼ cup (60 ml) extra virgin olive oil

Serves 6 | ⏲ Prep time: 70 minutes
Per serving approx.: 165 calories, 5 g protein, 12 g fat, 10 g carbohydrates

1   Soak raisins in vinegar for about 1 hour. Toast pine nuts until light brown.

2   Rinse spinach and place in a pot. Heat until spinach wilts, stirring occasionally, and drain.

3   Peel garlic and cut into thick slices. In a pan, heat oil, and sauté garlic, then remove from pan and set aside.

4   Drain raisins, add to pan with spinach, braise for about 7 minutes and season with salt and pepper. Serve sprinkled with garlic and pine nuts.

Potato Arugula Salad

1¾ lb (800 g) new potatoes | 3 oz (100 g) arugula | 3 oz (100 g) cucumber | 3 tbs extra virgin olive oil | 3 tbs hot vegetable stock | 3 tbs white wine vinegar | 1 tsp mild mustard | Kosher salt | Freshly ground black pepper | 1 green onion | 1 clove garlic

Serves 6 | ⏲ Prep time: 1 hour
Per serving approx.: 135 calories, 2 g protein, 6 g fat, 16 g carbohydrates

1   Rinse potatoes and cook in boiling salted water for about 20 minutes. Rinse arugula, sort, and tear into pieces. Rinse cucumber and dice finely.

2   Stir together oil, stock, vinegar, mustard, salt, and pepper. Rinse green onion, clean, chop into fine rings, and add. Peel garlic, squeeze through a press, and add.

3   Drain potatoes, peel while hot, and depending on size, cut into quarters or eighths. Mix with sauce. Fold in cucumber and arugula and marinate for 30 minutes before serving.

surprising!

Coconut Cauliflower

Wonderfully mild and with an Asian flair.

¼ cup (60 g) grated coconut | 7 oz (200 g) Greek yogurt | 2 tbs extra virgin olive oil | 1 tbs freshly squeezed lime juice | 2 tbs chopped cilantro | Kosher salt | Cumin | 14 oz (400 g) cleaned cauliflower florets | 2 tbs sesame seeds | Sugar

Serves 4 | ⏱ Prep time: 25 minutes
Per serving approx.: 245 calories, 4 g protein, 17 g fat, 4 g carbohydrates

1   In an ungreased pan, toast coconut until light brown and transfer to a bowl.

2   Add yogurt, oil, lime juice, and cilantro and stir. Season sauce to taste with salt, cumin, and, if desired, 1 pinch sugar.

3   Slice cauliflower florets and add to sauce. Season to taste with salt and cumin. In an ungreased pan, toast sesame seeds while stirring until they give off an aroma and sprinkle over cauliflower.

GOES WITH?
All Asian fondues, fish and shrimp in tempura batter, chicken stock.

inexpensive & fast

Hot Chili Cucumber

Fresh Asian ingredients provide a hot, aromatic accompaniment to meat and fish.

For the dressing
¼ cup (60 ml) heavy cream | 2 tbs yogurt | 1 tbs mild white wine vinegar | 2 pickled red chili peppers | 1 clove garlic | 3 sprigs mint | 1 pinch cumin | Kosher salt | Freshly ground pepper
Plus
1 small cucumber | 3 small tomatoes

Serves 4 | ⏱ Prep time: 20 minutes
Per serving approx.: 70 calories, 1 g protein, 5 g fat, 3 g carbohydrates

1   For the dressing, combine cream, yogurt, and vinegar. Slice chili peppers into fine rings and add. Peel garlic and chop finely. Rinse mint, shake dry, and cut leaves into fine strips. Add mint and garlic to dressing. Season to taste with cumin, salt, and pepper.

2   Rinse cucumber and grate coarsely. Rinse tomatoes, cut in half, remove cores, and dice finely. Add cucumber and tomatoes to dressing and stir. Season to taste with salt, pepper, and cumin.

GOES WITH?
Meat and fish fondues, as well as meat and fish deep-fried in batter.

Sweet Fondues

My family always welcomes chocolaty, fruity fondue for dessert.
But why not have a sweet fondue with Sunday coffee? In this case,
be sure to increase amounts by fifty percent.

Double Chocolate Dessert Fondue

3½ oz (100 g) milk chocolate
3½ oz (100 g) semi-sweet chocolate
3½ oz (100 g) heavy cream
1 pinch ground ginger
About 1¾ lb (800 g) fruit (cleaned or peeled,
  banana, apple, star fruit, mango, kiwi,
  strawberries, etc.)

Serves 4 (¾ cup or 175 ml) | ◎ Prep time:
15 minutes
Per serving approx.: 450 calories, 5 g protein,
24 g fat, 52 g carbohydrates

1 Break chocolate into small pieces. Place a ceramic pot on the stove and melt chocolate with cream and ginger over low heat.

2 Prepare fruit by rinsing, peeling, or removing pits and slicing into bite-sized pieces. Either prepare a separate plate of colorful fruit for each guest or arrange all fruit on two serving dishes.

TIP—DICING MANGO QUICKLY

Without peeling the mango, cut fruit away from both sides of the pit. With a small knife, cut into the inside of each half in a crisscross pattern without piercing the peel. Turn peel inside-out and cut off cubes close to the peel.

fancy | for a large group

Chocolate Fondue

We love to serve this exceptionally fine chocolate fondue to finish off a meal. But it's also a favorite of sweet-toothed children at birthday parties.

10½ oz (300 g) chocolate (milk, semisweet, or a combination)

¾ cup (175 ml) milk

⅓ cup (80 g) chopped almonds

3 tbs honey

2 tbs cocoa powder

1 pinch salt

About 1¾ lbs (800 g) fruit in bite-sized pieces (see fruit variations)

About 14 oz (400 g) ladyfingers, plain cookies, or macaroons

Serves 6 | ⊚ Prep time: 10 minutes
Per serving approx.: 740 calories, 14 g protein, 28 g fat, 109 g carbohydrates

1 Break chocolate into chunks. In a saucepan, combine milk and chocolate and melt on the stovetop over low heat while stirring.

2 Toast almonds until light brown. Add almonds, honey, cocoa powder, and salt to chocolate, keeping mixture just hot enough to be very runny. Pour into an earthenware chocolate fondue pot and place on fondue burner or tea warmer.

3 Use your fingers to dip cookies into the chocolate and a fork to dip fruit.

CHOCOLATE VARIATIONS

For adults, flavor chocolate with 1 tablespoon (or more if desired) instant coffee. For a white chocolate fondue, use white chocolate, eliminate honey and cocoa powder, and add ¼ cup (60 g) grated coconut. For especially rich chocolate, use heavy cream instead of milk.

FRUIT VARIATIONS

For an exotic, tropical fondue, use gooseberries, baby pineapple, kiwis, bananas, litchis (watch out for seeds), star fruit (looks very decorative), and fresh figs; for fondue with a European flair, use pears, apples, grapes, strawberries, and cherries; make orange fondue with mangos, peaches, apricots, oranges, and tangerines; for fall fondue, use plums, apples, red and green grapes, and pears; melon fondue: use a melon baller to make balls from various melons (watermelon, muskmelon, honeydew melon); dried fruit fondue, serve with an assortment of dried apricots, figs, apples, and pears.

GOES WITH?

Vanilla or other favorite ice cream flavors, coconut macaroons, cookies, angel food cake, or pound cake.

in crispy coconut batter

Pineapple Fondue

1 pineapple | Oil for deep-frying
For the batter
½ cup (125 ml) flour | ¼ cup (60 g) grated
coconut | ½ cup (125 ml) milk | 1 egg | 1 tsp oil

Serves 4–6 | ⊚ Prep time: 20 minutes
Per serving approx.: 280 calories, 11 g protein,
27 g fat, 53 g carbohydrates

1 Peel pineapple, cut lengthwise into quarters,
remove core, and cut into bite-sized pieces.
Arrange on two serving dishes.

2 Combine flour, coconut, milk, egg, and oil and
transfer batter to one large or two individual bowls.

3 Place oil in fondue pot and heat on the stovetop
to about 325°F (170°C) (see page 7). Transfer to
fondue burner. Spear pineapple with a fork, dip in
batter, and fry in oil until golden brown.

GOES WITH?
Cinnamon sugar, vanilla sauce and chocolate sprinkles,
chocolate sauce, or fruit compote.

VARIATIONS
Instead of pineapple, dip banana slices in coconut
batter and serve with chocolate sauce. Or try apples
instead of pineapple. In this case, replace grated
coconut with finely chopped hazelnuts and season
batter with a little cinnamon.

can prepare in advance

Crispy Cream Puffs

Port-Wine Fig Sauce
4 fresh figs | ¼ cup (60 g) sugar | ⅔ cup (150 ml)
port wine | ⅓ cup (75 ml) red wine | ¼ cup
(60 ml) orange juice | 1 pinch cardamom |
1 pinch cloves
Dough
3½ tbs (50 g) butter | 1 tbs sugar | 1 pinch salt |
⅔ cup (150 g) flour | 4 eggs | Oil for deep-frying |
Wire ladle

Serves 4 | ⊚ Prep time: 30 minutes |
Soaking time: 12 hours
Per serving approx.: 555 calories, 11 g protein,
27 g fat, 53 g carbohydrates

1 Pierce fig peels and place in a bowl. In a
saucepan, melt sugar in port and red wine and
briefly bring to a boil. Pour over figs, cover, and
soak overnight. Remove figs from liquid and purée
with ¼ cup (60 ml) liquid and orange juice. Season
to taste with cardamom and cloves. Transfer to
small bowls.

2 Combine 1 cup (250 ml) water, butter, sugar,
and salt; bring to a boil and remove from heat.
Vigorously beat in flour until smooth and continue
stirring until dough comes away from the sides of
the pan in a ball. Remove from heat and vigorously
beat in eggs one at a time. Place dough on a
serving dish.

3 Place fondue pot on stovetop and heat oil to
325°F (170°C). Transfer to fondue burner. Scoop
small balls from dough and, depending on their
size, fry for 5–7 minutes, flipping over once.
Remove with a slotted spoon.

also delicious with other fruit sauces

Cream Puffs with Strawberry Banana Sauce

Fry the little scraps of dough that are left behind after scooping out cream puffs.

½ cube yeast (¾ oz or 21 g) | ⅓ cup (75 g) sugar | 1½ cups (330 g) flour | 1 pinch salt | 2 egg yolks | ¼ cup (60 g) butter | 1 tbs rum | ¾ cup (175 ml) milk | 1 lb (450 g) strawberries | 1 medium-sized banana | Flour for the work surface | Oil for deep-frying

Serves 4–6 | ⏱ Prep time: 20 minutes |
Rising time: 30 minutes
Per serving (6) approx.: 500 calories, 9 g protein, 22 g fat, 63 g carbohydrates

1   Crumble yeast, mix with 2 tablespoons sugar, and let dissolve. Combine flour, salt, egg yolk, butter, rum, yeast, and milk and knead vigorously. Let rise in a warm place for about 30 minutes, kneading once.

2   On a floured work surface, roll out dough to a thickness of about ¾ inch (2 cm). Cut dough into circles (about ¾ inch (2 cm) diameter). Arrange on a serving dish.

3   Rinse and clean strawberries, peel banana, chop fruit coarsely, and purée with remaining sugar.

4   Place fondue pot on stovetop and heat oil to 325°F (170°C) (see page 7). Using a spoon, transfer cream puffs one at a time to hot oil and fry for 2–3 minutes until brown then flip over, and brown for 3 more minutes.

VARIATION—WITH APPLE
Finely dice 1 medium-sized apple and knead into dough. If desired, season with a little cinnamon.

Blueberry Yogurt Sauce

7 oz (200 g) blueberries | 8 oz (250 g) plain
yogurt | 2 tbs (30 g) honey | 1 tbs powdered sugar
| 1 tbs (2 cl) Crème de Cassis (optional)

Makes about 1¼ cup (300 ml) | ◎ Prep time:
10 minutes
Per serving approx.: 100 calories, 2 g protein,
2 g fat, 16 g carbohydrates

1   Rinse blueberries and drain, setting aside about
¼ cup (60 g).

2   In a blender, purée remaining blueberries
with all ingredients. Stir in blueberries that were
set aside.

TIPS

This sauce is relatively runny and goes well with Crispy
Cream Puffs (see page 56). For thicker sauce, replace
half the yogurt with sour cream. Prepare sauce with
blueberries or blackberries, but in this case purée
separately and pass through a strainer before adding
to yogurt. If desired, flavor with vanilla.

Orange Mango Sauce

¾ cup (175 ml) blood orange juice (or freshly
squeezed orange juice) | 3–4 tbs (50 g) sugar |
Fruit from ½ ripe mango | 1 tbs cornstarch
Makes about 1 cup (125 ml) | ◎ Prep time:
15 minutes
Per serving approx.: 95 calories, 0 g protein,
1 g fat, 22 g carbohydrates

1   In a blender, purée orange juice, sugar, and
mango. Transfer to a saucepan and bring to a boil.

2   Stir cornstarch into a little cold water. Stir into
purée, briefly bring to a boil, and reduce while
stirring. Serve warm or cold.

TIP

If a ripe mango is not available, substitute 1 cup (125 ml)
freshly squeezed orange juice. This sauce is especially
quick to make if using juice from the store.

Using this Index
To help find recipes containing certain ingredients quickly, this index lists favorite ingredients (such as fruit or arugula) in alphabetical order and bold type, followed by the corresponding recipes.

Thank you!
A special thanks to the Silit company for providing the fondue sets and accessories in this book.

Published originally under the title Fondues © 2006 Gräfe und Unzer Verlag GmbH, Munich. English translation for the U.S. market © 2007, Silverback Books, Inc.

Program director: Doris Birk
Managing editor: Birgit Rademacker
Editor: Ruth Wiebusch, Lynda Zuber Sassı
Reader: Maryna Zimdars
Layout, typography and cover design: Independent Medien Design, Munich
Typesetting: Liebl Satz+Grafik, Emmering
Translation: Christy Tam
Production: Petra Roth, Patty Holden
Reproduction: Penta Repro, Munich
Printing and binding: Appl, Wemding

Printed in China

ISBN-10: 1-59637-235-4
ISBN-13: 978-1-59637-235-1

The Author
Claudia Lenz is an ecotrophologist and freelance author and editor. In developing her recipes, her focus is on dishes for uncomplicated every-day cooking. The original impetus for this book came from the opulent, traditional fondue feast served by her friend Ute and—an essential ingredient for implementing the project—Gudrun Mach's participation as recipe tester and expert on sweet fondues.

The Photographer
Klaus-Maria Einwanger is an independent photographer in Rosenheim, Germany. He works for magazines, prestigious publishers and advertising agencies both at home and abroad. With creativity and authenticity, he presents perfect images of food specialties from around the world. For this project, he also had the enthusiastic support of Daniel Petri, food stylist.

Photo Credits
Cover photo: Joerg Lehmann, Paris
All other photos: Klaus-Maria Einwanger, Rosenheim

Enjoy these Quick & Easy Books in their new format

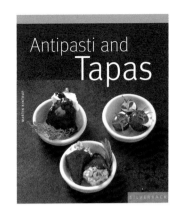

Antipasti and Tapas

Fondue

Herbs and Spices

Raclette

Salad

Sushi

Waffles

1   2   3

It Pays to Plan Ahead

1 Dishes

Most commercially available fondue sets allow up to 6 people to comfortably stick their forks into the pot. If you're planning on serving a larger group, you will need more than one pot. For each guest, set the table with a fondue plate or shallow dish—it doesn't have to be very big—a knife, fork, fondue fork, and, if appropriate, a slotted spoon. For the fondue ingredients, you'll need serving utensils and platters, bread baskets, and small bowls for sauces. Depending on the fondue and ingredients, you may need salad bowls and saucers covered with paper towels for draining fried foods.

2 Prepare a variety

To really succeed, a meat or vegetable fondue must exhibit a certain variety, both visual and culinary. For example, three sauces are enough and seven is too many. Prepare sauces hours ahead of time, or even the day before, cover them with plastic wrap, and refrigerate. Transfer any pickled ingredients and less sensitive raw vegetables to serving dishes in advance, cover, and refrigerate until it is time to serve. Salad and dressing can also be prepared ahead of time; wait to dress salad just before serving.

3 A few thoughts about wine

A classic fondue is impossible without wine! But what type of wine? For cheese to melt correctly and blend, you need a good white wine that is sufficiently acidic. Suitable white wine grapes include, Riesling, Pinot Blanc/White Burgundy, Sauvignon Blanc, or Chenin Blanc.Taste a few before making a decision. Be sure to buy a generous amount—after a period of dunking and bubbling on the burner, cheese fondue could usually do with a refill—as could your guests!